THE HUMBLE

HUSTLER

WHERE HUSTLING AND ENTREPRENEURSHIP COINCIDES

Copyright © 2021 by HLK Management Inc.

First paperback edition December 2021

Photography & Graphic design by GVUCreative
Contribution by Nicole Antoine

ISBN 978-1-7778545-0-8 (paperback)

www.thehumblehustler.com

DEDI CATIONS

This book is dedicated to the current, past and future hustlers worldwide. Know that you are an entrepreneur at heart, that you are limitless and that you are the grassroots of your nation's economy. My hope is that this handbook serves as a tool for your many endeavors. May the jewels resonate in your mind like your favorite song.

To my children, may your spirit embrace and grasp the concept of The Humble Hustler. May it stir you into becoming wealth builders. I wish you never have to work for money but rather create a stream where many can earn. Like the grandfather tree in the forest, I hope that you navigate this world with an immune system armed to the teeth with the knowledge and wisdom I've acquired for us. May you win, especially when you lose. I pray that you will be blessed with humility, discernment and understanding. And to the uttermost hustler/entrepreneur I've ever met – my mother. I watched you hustle in silence. You raised us, worked your career, worked your side hustle into a retirement plan for all of whom you support and created a diversified real estate portfolio. If I knew then what I know now, I would've followed you, listened more, saved time, and saved myself the heartaches and growing pains of entrepreneurship.

ACKNOW LEDGEMENTS

Salute to every hustler I've ever met, dealt with directly or indirectly. Honest or dishonest, fed or state time, on the road or in the grave. We crossed paths for a reason, and our encounter helped mold me into who I am today. To the kings I've built with that came home and regained their thrones. To hip-hop, a global culture that raised so many of us. You've turned idlers and street runners into poets and teachers. You showed us what Meech should've been and what Supreme didn't become. To the women – mother of civilization and architects to all hustles known to man. Our train of thought is mainly based on you; therefore, together, we can redesign our thinking patterns and our dreams and engineer a whole new way of life. The world is yours. Know your power, your role and most of all your worth.

Instruction to the reader

1. Musical Jewels : Information rich in valuable knowledge coded through lyrical word play.
2. Jewelry : Subtle coded information rich in knowledge applicable throughout one's life these words are identified in **"bold"**.
3. Exhibits : Applicable challenges for the reader to participate in.

PRE ACE

Throughout the history of humankind, storytelling has been a form of history transmission. Our DNA, heritage and environment reveal parts of our story. Similar to music. A good artist is a good storyteller, and through words, can transport you through their story and reality. I learned about similes and metaphors in school, but through hip-hop, my ears perked at the sound of *"double entendres."* Double entendres have different meanings depending on the listener's knowledge of the topic. For example, an artist can say a verse that you heard and recited at fifteen while riding the *cheese bus,* and you can repeat the same verse fifteen years later and have a different understanding of the message. I'm still trying to figure out how this phenomenon is so underrated on a global scale. The truth is that we live in a world of "double entendres."

Take my life, for example – my tales as an athlete, hustler and entrepreneur coincide in so many ways. Simply put, *hustling* is getting active and making something out of nothing. Depending on the demographic in the room, the term "hustle" can be tossed around and have different meanings. I added the word hustler as one of my titles not only to define my work ethic but to describe an occupation. This handbook details some of my hard-learned lessons and successes in all three paths that I've chosen. Life is a mini-series filled with all kinds of challenges. Entrepreneurship is available to all ages, races and genres. With time steadily evading us, the cost of doing business is always in question, often bringing one's flexibility to the test. Knowledge, wisdom and understanding are necessities.

To all hustlers, ballers, players, pitchers, soldiers, plugs, outlets, pipelines, plumbers, herbalists, middlemen, masons and bricklayers – regardless of the hustle hat you choose to wear, corporate or underground, allow this handbook to serve as your *consigliere.*

CHALLENGE

How many *DOUBLE ENTENDRES* were in this preface?

chapter 1 ONE'S OPPORTUNITY COST

In a time where the average citizen's income stream has been altered or halted by a worldwide pandemic, we've seen people suffer through a period plagued by fear and uncertainty. Some made noise about their government's duties to assist, while some strapped up and got their hustle on. Circumstances beyond our control gave way to a level playing field of *opportunity cost*.

The truth is, nothing changed for the hustlers. Making something out of nothing is part of our foundation. With tough times weaved into our DNA, anything short of the world's end is gravy to us. While people panicked, we plotted and recognized that our lifestyle was a talent that couldn't be sold. ›››

The hustler and the entrepreneur have a relationship similar to two homies from the same block attending different schools. Their ciphers and swagger intertwine. The only difference is the school building. The same goes for the hustler and the entrepreneur – in a slight change of outfit or surroundings, you can no longer tell them apart. That is because, at the core, they are identical.

Opportunity cost is a layered equation that appears in every decision the hustler makes. It takes time to understand and years of experience to master. For example, the phone rings for a $4k move that requires six hour drive. Leaving equates to missing out on today's opportunity to pull in $1.5k locally. The four stacks seem enticing and simple but the true value amounts to an extra $2.5k. Still worth it, right? Dollar-wise maybe, but factoring in basic opportunity cost, every journey away from home turf presents its challenges, and the hustler has to assess things a lot further. Opportunity cost has multiple facets that go beyond dollar signs. Peace of mind and certainty of working with legit allies versus stepping into new terrain is a figureless comparison. *Pilots check for friendly skies before flying. We also must check the temperature before packing.* Risk assessment is an innate part of our survival.

What's it all worth to you? $100k can be pennies or millions to the next man. There is no right or wrong answer. The truth lies within yourself. Only you know the type of hustler you are and the risk you can manage. But it's a lot harder to establish a true legacy while your primary concern is survival. For me, dodging the pen and graveyard for as long as possible was essential. As an entrepreneur, I now look to extend my core values into all my projects which is way more profitable than surviving. ›››

Sound Jewels

In a hip-hop song titled "U Don't Know" by Jay-Z, the artist consciously assesses his opportunity cost by weighing that a key could generate 40k. However, a developed skill set in songwriting and rhyming could surpass that amount without jeopardizing one's safety.

The game is rich in lessons with a twist of selfishness. It's a tough juggle. Although we think we are playing alone, we involve our family by association. A responsible hustler will factor that into his opportunity cost at all times. Safety is one thing, but there's no measuring stick for the emotional rollercoaster we force upon our family. We've seen families destroyed behind bad opportunity cost management. How ironic is that? The people you think you're hustling for could end up bearing the worst kind of stress brought on by the game you chose. Regardless of your work field, balance is required. Are we working to live or living to work? If so, at what cost?

I've had wise women in my life walk away from our relationship in protest of my lifestyle. I've had good women ride with me while trying to steer me away from it, and I've had others stay quiet and out of my business. Unfortunately, my relationships were a casualty of my lifestyle, similar to Michael Corleone losing Kate as his empire grew in the Godfather saga. When our obsessive ambition for success plays against us, those we love often suffer the most.›››

FAMILY AFFAIR

Sound Jewels

In the hustler's mind, all he's doing outside is bringing food to the table and doesn't understand his significant other's worries and concerns. People who work a regular job and view street hustling as the easy route misunderstand how complicated and intricate that lifestyle truly is. Hustlers didn't create that selected path out of looking for something easy but rather for something more than society's middle-class lifestyle. Lil Wayne's "Hustler Musik" and Jay-Z's "D'Evils" both express similar sentiments on the subject matter.

HINDSIGHT

Simply put, opportunity cost is what you lose on the flip side of every choice you make. It can be a monetary gain versus a personal loss or vice versa. As a hustler, I wasn't content with my so-called opportunities, which led me to create my own at all costs. Factoring opportunity cost in my decision-making process would've made me a better hustler, a better entrepreneur and a better person. Nowadays, I do not make a move without it being in the equation. It keeps me accountable for my actions and fills in the cracks in my armour where ego and pride could set in. Knowing then what I know now would've saved me a lot of grief, but then again, I wouldn't have acquired the knowledge necessary to write this handbook. Brokers, consultants, creators, stylists, barbers, artists, etc.; all need to view themselves as their own business and calculate their opportunity cost in order to achieve their goals without leaving a disaster behind.

Exhibit A
Opportunity Cost Board

Every opportunity has a cost. That is a fact. Regretfully, some of us calculate it, and some don't. Many so-called hustlers opt to rob you for what they can get now versus what they stand to make by working with you in the long run. Some also choose to leave a career path for another without knowing what lies ahead for them. Let us utilize this tool to gather a numerical perspective for every path chosen.

- The first column shows an occupation, the time required (9-5), its daily rewards and risks.
- The second column shows a side hustle, time you have to put aside for it, its daily rewards and risks.
- The third column shows a second side hustle, time required, its daily rewards and risks.

This chart is a basic visual of opportunity cost in comparison from a career standpoint versus a side hustle. You can use the graph to give yourself a break-even point and a goal as to where your side hustle has to reach to cover and surpass your initial opportunity cost. Keeping in mind the time, risks and profits, this board will allow you to make decisions without blindsiding yourself. Financial freedom is the goal. Evading risk while generating the most income in the least amount of time possible is a simple way to make opportunity cost work in your favor.

Exhibit A.1

	Occupation - Barbering -	Side Hustle A - Catering -	Side Hustle B - Finessing -
Times required	9am-6pm (9hrs)	7am-12pm	Months of homework
Daily rewarded	$250 - $400	$300-$500	One big hit for a couple thousands
Risk/Cost	Mobility and lack of attention to my other hustles	Initial food and packaging costs.	Looking over your shoulder for years to come.

Exhibit A.2
I've provided an empty chart for you to visualize and work
on your own opportunity cost.

	Occupation	Side Hustle A	Side Hustle B
Times required			
Daily rewarded			
Risk/Cost			

chapter 2 **FATHER TIME**

"Prisons and cemeteries are filled with people who made bad split second decisions"
-Coach G.-

Time is considered fatherly for its disciplinary ways. It teaches lessons and heals wounds simultaneously. For hustlers, Father Time is the ultimate referee. There is no use debating it. Once a call is made, arguing will only cost you more time which is a vital currency. Having it taken away teaches us that. Day 1 of my *bit* appeared to be my longest day ever. No clock in sight and no way of knowing how much confinement time was ahead. The arrest played over and over in my mind. ›››

Thoughts of variables out of my control slowed my clock all the way down and caused me to do **bad time.** Yes, there is such a thing as good and bad time while doing a stint in the **belly of the beast.** Good time can be profitable, filling your mind with knowledge-seeking wisdom and discovering valuable information to **overstand** the world's ways. Training your body, pushing through limits you thought were insurmountable while getting to know yourself. These missions set off a different timer inside me, taking power away from the system and my sentence. Bad time can be exhausting as your mind fills with realities out of your control which will most likely lead to anger, stress and/or depression. I chose to own my situation and use my time to better myself on all levels, so the judge and his gavel became powerless to me and my goals. I was on a personal wellness journey sponsored by the Feds.

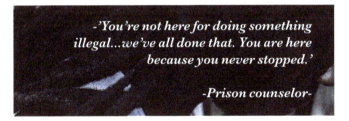

-'You're not here for doing something illegal...we've all done that. You are here because you never stopped.'

-Prison counselor-

Similar to corporate bonuses being private, time is a personal matter not discussed inside. Once I had a release date, I kept it to myself out of respect for those catching L's and others not as **short** as me. Short time usually slows down the clock as well. Not only do others stay clear of short-timers for their sanity, but the mind starts living on the outside again. To speed up such an inevitable process, I gave myself the most wide-ranging to-do list possible. Ten books in four months, or no phone time! By doing so, I was able to replace my release date with a deliverable mission. I went from my longest day ever to now running out of time inside! Can you believe it? The mind is our most powerful tool, and this is an example of how I controlled time instead of letting it control me. That strategy is being utilized in business more so today. Companies now realize that people can be way more productive while aiming at a deliverable goal versus a time scheduled ending. Many institutions were forced to lock down and found out this truth organically. Employees working from the comfort of their homes have proven to be more productive with a full itinerary to tackle rather than a predetermined start and finish time. ›››

CLOCK WORK

Real hustlers never really appear to be panicking during time constraints. For us, keeping calm while problem-solving is second nature. Time management is a subconscious skill that comes with the territory since we are all on borrowed time anyway. These circumstances are partly the reason why we develop a second clock. On the one hand, we have the world clock, which operates with time zones and is reflected on your phone. On the other hand, the hustler has an inner clock that sets its own time – influenced by emotions, our notion of time is often sped up or slowed down according to how we feel at the moment. Fun times appear to go by faster than hard times. Depending on the situation, chasing time makes it speed up and run out on you, while waiting on time feels like it slowed down on purpose. ›››

Being that hustlers and entrepreneurs set their hours, they mostly operate on the second clock. We have been setting our work, eat and sleep hours ever since choosing the self-employed route. Time and opportunity cost go together. What we do with our time is what sets our salary. Hustling has no salary cap, but sleeping in has a price as the next hustler works day and night. Depending on your hustle, sleeping period equals loss of revenue. So to save time, we eat while conducting business, take naps when it's quiet and date someone flexible. ›››

Sound Jewels

In the song titled "Streets Is Watching" Jay-Z describes himself as an earner in a game filled with outsiders plotting to take what's yours. While debating how to handle it, his turning point is the time allocated for getting caught if something went wrong. Several years worth way too much in dollar signs for him.

THE GAMBLER

Good hustlers also develop the ability to tell time without a watch. Knowing when it's time to switch up your hustle, location, marketing, and strategy is key. The opportunity cost will help you iron out which play to make against what risk. However, knowing or not knowing the time can be the difference between you being a bishop or a pawn.

The referee makes the calls we can't dispute. However, the seasoned hustler who knows time can anticipate them and move accordingly. This could mean positioning ourselves in favor of those calls or simply bracing ourselves for its impact. Either way, keeping the element of surprise off the table can only be viewed as a positive. The popular phrase claiming that 'knowing is half the battle' is an understatement to entrepreneurs. More often than none, knowing is the battle! Information is a key tool that can be the difference between a thriving or a losing business. The hustler that knows better will most likely end up doing better. ▪

Sound Jewels

In this game of life, we've all been dealt a particular hand. Knowing when and what to nurture, take with us or leave in the past is what sets us apart. Every situation has some values. You must choose what's valuable to you and for how long. Kenny Rogers' song "The Gambler" depicted this rule perfectly.

Exhibit B
Disciplinary board

Even under Father Time's terms, a day is equal to twenty-four hours for all of us. No one can say they've had more or less time than anyone else in a day. How we use our time separates most of us from where we are to where we want to be. We all have things we like doing and things that need doing. No motivation or discipline is required for us to do what we like doing. The problems usually come when we gotta tackle the things we need to do. Success will likely come to those who attack their list of needs with the same love they have for their list of wants. Below, I've written down two lists separating them between 'needs' and 'wants' to develop that skill. I would then apply self-discipline and prohibit myself from enjoying any activity on the 'wants' list until my 'needs' list was completed. This game would set off my second clock organically, causing me to knock out my list of needs to enjoy my list of wants. Eventually, when my 'wants' list starts mirroring my 'needs' list the process becomes fun and second nature. My twenty-four hours is now filled with a list of missions gearing me up towards success.

- The first column shows a list of things I have to do, and not necessarily enjoy (workout, meal prep, work on a project, read a book, meditate.)

- The second column shows a list of things I love doing for fun and entertainment (Dominos/cards, eating out, sleeping in, having sex, watch a show.)

"Needs" list	Done	"Wants" list	Done
Meditation		Play Dominos	
Workout		Sleep in	
Project Development		Watch my favorite shows	
Spend time with significant other		Have sex	

Exhibit B.1

I've provided an empty board for you. Fill in your own list of activities and compare your wants to your needs. You'll be aligned in no time.

"Needs" list	Done	"Wants" list	Done

chapter 3

WATER FALL

An open-ended opportunity cost and an unwavering referee clocking every movement are some of the circumstances that mold the hustler's state of mind. Even though the treacherous playing field is far from leveled, success is attainable by rocking with the waves and becoming the current. We take on different personas, positions and hustles depending on our environment. The heights we rise to and fall from could trouble anyone not accustomed to this lifestyle. In this unpredictable cycle, we're forced to adopt the attributes of water. We learn to be formless and develop the ability to adapt to any temperature. Our rock-solid state is a result of the frigid climate, just as the summer weather has us in free flowing mode. Group us in harmony, and we'll create a phenomenal site – as gorgeous as a waterfall or as threatening as a tsunami. We deal with transformation and continuation rather than elimination. ›››

FLEXIBILITY

Water flows with no ownership and isn't married to any one form. Its free streams take on the shapes and properties directed by its environment. The double-edged sword called commitment can be so rewarding and penalizing at the same time. Surely, a lack of commitment in anything will guarantee a mediocre outcome. But in business, too much commitment in a specific direction can also lead to our demise. Can we imagine a hot African sun beaming on an icicle without melting it? Or if Antarctica's weather was unable to sustain its glaciers? Entrepreneurs can put down a plan destined for execution. Circumstances along the way will require free-flowing and rock-solid tendencies. The flexibility of water and its lack of commitment to any one specific form is what we are after. Being too stubborn or married to an initial plan can be a mistake. The Hustler inside will take on the necessary measures to achieve the goal. Put on the uniform required for this task, take on the required shape to keep moving forward. Being overly committed can equate to tunnel vision, which can cause us to miss out on key adjustments essential to succeed. ›››

"Be formless. Shapeless. Like water. You put water into a cup. It becomes the cup. Water can flow or it can crash. Be water, my friend."

- Bruce Lee -

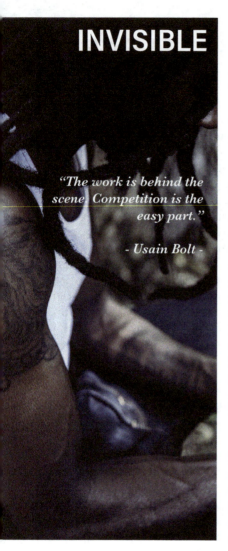

INVISIBLE

"The work is behind the scene. Competition is the easy part."

- Usain Bolt -

One of water's many properties is that it is felt but not seen. Humidity is the concentration of water present in the atmosphere. Water is around us at all times, especially when it manages to bind with oxygen in gas form. In a similar fashion, a hustlers' existence relies heavily on the groundwork done in private. The grind we put in while no one is looking determines the picture shown when the cameras are rolling. The underground foundation of a building is what determines the possible size of the tower. The humble hustler moves in silence, putting down the foundation with passion and grit while no one is looking. The magic happens when no one can see it – free of scrutiny and public opinion. Anyone can be motivated by an attentive crowd. The skill set of self-motivation in private cannot be sold or duplicated.

Entrepreneurs are the chameleons of the business world. Our ability to turn a profit out of whatever comes in our crosshair makes it hard to put us in a box. But we can and will fit in any box until something else comes along, or the weather changes. Then we'll naturally make our adjustment and take on the necessary shape. We are limitless individuals in a limitless industry. »»

"To improve is to change; to be perfect is to change often."

-Winston Churchill-

NATURAL DISASTERS

As beautiful and soothing as water can be, it is also responsible for its share of damage on this planet. Where beauty and terror intertwine, so do success and failure in entrepreneurship. No matter how prepared we think we are when water commences on a destructive path, nothing man-made can stop it. Tsunamis and hurricanes have torn throughout countries worldwide since the beginning of time. A nation's ability to rebuild itself is how we measure its efficiency. Not if it could avoid the inevitable. Failure is a humbling experience and a necessary teacher. Surviving today's trials and tribulations is what prepares us for tomorrow's success and accolades. If failure makes you sick or you classify losing as a bad experience, then the entrepreneurial world isn't for you. It is too unpredictable and merciless. This life is for those who live for the thrill, and enjoy the journey for its highs and lows. It's for the go-getters that plan their bounce back as their skin touches the canvas.

No manual can make your journey failproof. The aim is to develop the hustler's ability to regroup and take on any shape or form while aiming fearlessly at a new endeavor. Some of us swam the oceans searching for *fish scales*. We view soft waters as easier to navigate, correct? Salt or soft waters both carry their separate challenges. The games and parameters vary, but the rules remain the same. Mastering the art of adjusting remains our only challenge. ▪

Sound Jewels

On his debut album Reasonable Doubt, Jay-Z's " Can I Live " resonates with the hustler's state of mind with a similar comparison to nature and the need to remain on an even keel regardless of the highs or lows.

Exhibit C
Less is more

Water is everywhere around us in multiple forms. Limitless yet disciplined at the same time. Felt even when unseen. A significant part of the Humble Hustler's concept is adopting water's properties while maneuvering through unpredictable situations. Those same properties can and will serve you once applied in the entrepreneurial world. Multiply your hustles and revenue streams. Play different positions within your scheme to win. Personal change is an uncomfortable process, but most times, it is a necessary one to progress. (i.e. I want a profitable stock portfolio and two vacations a year.

I'll have to become passionate about the stocks and bonds game, cut down on my social life and learn what the pros of that field already know. If I'm not in love with reading, that's going to have to change. Meditate on the subject matter. Being a loner, I'll have to go against my nature and congregate with the players already striving in that game. And I will challenge myself to have my vacations paid for by my stock profits!)

Some of us cannot sit still long enough to let the current of success guide us home. Others have only one property of water and struggle to make adjustments. Erase all limits and write down water's properties that you would need to adopt to unlock your full potential as an entrepreneur.

I've provided writing space for you to jot down some ideas or notes to return to.

_____

_____

_____

_____

_____

_____

_____

_____

_____

_____

_____

_____

_____

_____

_____

CON CLUSION

"The Game tickets are expensive right off the rip, courtside and nosebleed seats cost about the same."

- O.G. -

In a nutshell, the entrepreneur is the hustler gone pro! We earned Bachelor's degrees in Opportunity Cost and Risk Assessment, a Master's in Time Management and a Ph.D. in the Art of Change. Some hustles timed out, and many hustlers withered away instead of adjusting or evolving. There were profitable hustles in the 90's, others in the 2000s and so on. A select few packed light and brought the right tools into the next game and never looked back. They weren't stuck on any ideology. They committed to being the change and became entrepreneurs. ›››

If life brought us lemons? Lemonade would be the furthest thing on the list of what we'd do with it. We've made juice with way less. Most of us weren't given anything and figured out a way to create our lane. Many hustlers are simply one degree of separation away – one door, one collaboration, one conversation or one adjustment away from being multi-figure earners. Part of why hustlers rapidly climb the ranks in every field they enter is that they carry attributes acquired from previous games. True principles can crossover in any genre. Survival in one can equate to significant success in the next.

"Humble hustlers are the type to pay the plug in full regardless of circumstances. Takes a different kind of character to do that."

- Rome -

So who is the hustler? The term represents the migrant having to build from scratch in a place far from home. The college student who works or plays sports to cover tuition. The parent(s) juggling work and a few side hustles, so their children lack for nothing. The providers who put the needs of the family above their own. The convicted felon released into a society no longer favorable for their success. A person who decided the parameters set for his or her existence was too narrow and created their own. The hustler's ways are in so many of us, either by circumstance or pure ambition. My question is, do you recognize yourself yet?

CLOSING REMARKS

Take this time to search deep within yourself and express your inner most real wants for yourself. There is power in the ability to dream, and the first course of action is to translate it into the physical world by writing it down. Whom you want to be, which position you want, and how you want to live. Own it, claim it, write it down and then become it.

"...people really do shape their lives through their thoughts."

- Robert T. Kiyosaki -

August 3rd, 2015. Last day of captivity although I never felt captured. Mixed feelings takeover me. Are there many more set up artists out there waiting for me? Can I succeed again? Will I be able to provide for myself again? But I'm filled with other emotions such as confidence, pride and strength. I wouldn't bet a dollar or a billion dollars against me. Life is good. Family is great and God is all the above. Now I know myself and Him. Wouldn't want to be outside the bubble on this on. Game on and I'm the biggest gamer there is. Jail didn't destroy me, I've defeated my enemies and confronted my fears. On August 4th, a fearless intelligently criminal minded individual with the strength of a pro athlete, and the ambition of a billionaire. Is RELEASED

JEWELRY / GLOSSARY

Jewelry : subtle information that helps to acquire
knowledge on one's path through life.

Double entendre — **CHAPTER :** PREFACE
definition : A word with an obvious definition that carries a secondary meaning to those with understanding in a different subject matter.

Cheese bus — **CHAPTER :** PREFACE
definition : Yellow school bus in charge of children and adolescents' travel to and from school.

Hustling — **CHAPTER :** PREFACE
definition : Being active, creative and aggressive while pursuing a goal.

Consigliere — **CHAPTER :** PREFACE
definition : An advisor to a person in a position of power.

The Game — **CHAPTER :** ONE
definition : A form of competitive play with established rules where one can win through skill, strength and luck. Also a street sport with very little to no rules where survival determines your wins and losses.

Hustler — **CHAPTER :** ONE
definition : An aggressive go-getter with unlimited ceiling space

Entrepreneur — **CHAPTER :** ONE
definition : A businessman with a high financial risk threshold.

Pilots check for friendly skies before flying, we also must check the temperature before packing. — **CHAPTER :** ONE
definition : Safety requirements in the sky corroborating with safety precautions during street business.

Key

definition : Mostly known as an instrument used to unlock doors, also used to describe a pivotal piece of information. In the game, used to describe a kilogram of a certain substance.

Finessing

definition : To out-wit someone in a very delicate manner for their goods usually with promises and lies that you know will never be fulfilled.

Overstand

definition : Understanding more than basic knowledge; mastering a topic

Prisons and cemeteries are filled with people who made bad split second decisions. - Coach G.

definition : A decision does not define you, but some bad decisions are irreversible. Life presents us with many scenarios where a split second determines our fate.

Bit

definition : Bit (pronounced 'bid') describes a prison sentence. Psychologically characterized as a minor punishment that one can handle with no problem.

Bad time

definition: Being in a bad emotional, mental or physical state while locked in the belly of the beast. The need to be in a good space in these three dimensions of wellness while dealing with a prison sentence is underrated and causes inmates to do time filled with worry and stress.

L'

definition : Used to categorize an inmate with a lifelong bit ahead or a major loss.

Belly of the beast

definition : Term used to describe an unpleasant place, most often referring to a prison

Short

definition : Usually used to describe a prison sentence that is winding down to its end. Being short varies amongst inmates and depends on the full length of the sentence. It can be anywhere from three years to three months.

"You aren't here for doing something illegal, we've all done that.
You are here because you never stopped !"
Prison counselor

definition : *Insinuating that everyone in the world has broken a rule of some sort at some point in time. Choosing to make it a career is the mistake, significantly altering one's odds of staying out of prison.*

"To improve is to change; to be perfect is to change often."
- Winston Churchill

definition : *Expect change in any area looking to be improved. Perfection is elusive and requires many frequent adjustments.*

"The work is behind the scenes. Competition is the easy part."
- Usain Bolt

definition : *We aren't privy to the work ethic, toll and commitment invested by the athlete/hustler/ entrepreneur to reach their goal. Our proof is usually the tangible outcome of the project/event.*

Fish scales

definition : *The sparkly outer layer of the fish in the ocean. Term is also used when referring to sparkly, and raw uncut cocaine.*

"The game tickets are expensive right off the rip, courtside and nosebleed
seats cost about the same."
- O.G.

definition : *The level of pressure and stress the street world brings to its participants and their families is high. Block kid, acting plug or kingpin all come in paying about the same initial cost regardless of their position on the totem pole.*

"Humble hustlers are the type to pay ——— *CHAPTER:* CONCLUSION
the Plug in full regardless of circumstances.
Takes a different kind of character to do that."
- Rome

definition: The Humble Hustler highlights a situation where most of us reach a crossroad. Paying consignment even when you lost sets many of us apart.

"...people really do shape their ——— *CHAPTER:* CLOSING REMARKS
lives through their thoughts."
- Robert T. Kiyosaki

definition: The acclaimed author of Rich Dad Poor Dad reflects on when he realized that we could mold our reality and our thoughts ourselves.

Slasher ——————————————— *CHAPTER:* ABOUT THE AUTHOR

definition: Term to describe a basketball player's ability to get in and out of lanes. Also the nickname of the Pittsburgh Steelers quarterback Kordell "Slash" Stewart for the number of positions he was capable of playing. Co-relation to all hustlers/entrepreneurs playing more than one role.

Alphabet Boys ————————————— *CHAPTER:* ABOUT THE AUTHOR

definition: Nickname given to American Federal task forces with letters on their jackets such as the Bureau of Alcohol, Tobacco and Firearms (ATF), Drug Enforcement Administration (DEA) and Federal Bureau of Investigation (FBI).

ABOUT THE AUTHOR

This ball-playing *slasher* crossed into many lanes as a hustler and entrepreneur. He harvested humility through the highs and lows of his journey, to which he credits much for his survival. With contacts from coast to coast, his hustles reached many borders. While dealing with so many hustlers, he was a target of the *alphabet boys,* which led him to do a bit for his involvement in a recorded conversation. With chips stacked on both sides of the win/loss column, this humble hustler is not one to play the victim. Rome has chosen to win even in a loss. His experiences gave way for an opportunity to enlighten young and old hustlers/entrepreneurs out there and give them some jewels to carry on their road to success. ▪

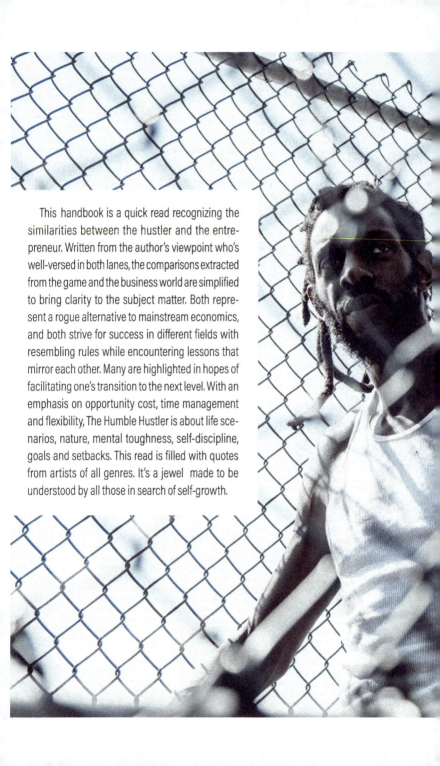

This handbook is a quick read recognizing the similarities between the hustler and the entrepreneur. Written from the author's viewpoint who's well-versed in both lanes, the comparisons extracted from the game and the business world are simplified to bring clarity to the subject matter. Both represent a rogue alternative to mainstream economics, and both strive for success in different fields with resembling rules while encountering lessons that mirror each other. Many are highlighted in hopes of facilitating one's transition to the next level. With an emphasis on opportunity cost, time management and flexibility, The Humble Hustler is about life scenarios, nature, mental toughness, self-discipline, goals and setbacks. This read is filled with quotes from artists of all genres. It's a jewel made to be understood by all those in search of self-growth.

CPSIA information can be obtained
at www.ICGtesting.com
Printed in the USA
LVHW081912191121
703873LV00008B/272